This coloring book is dedicated to my girl,
Abigail Grace, who is passionate about the
welfare and well-being of all animals, large and
small. Follow your dreams, baby girl, the
animals need more people like you;
especially your beloved elephants.

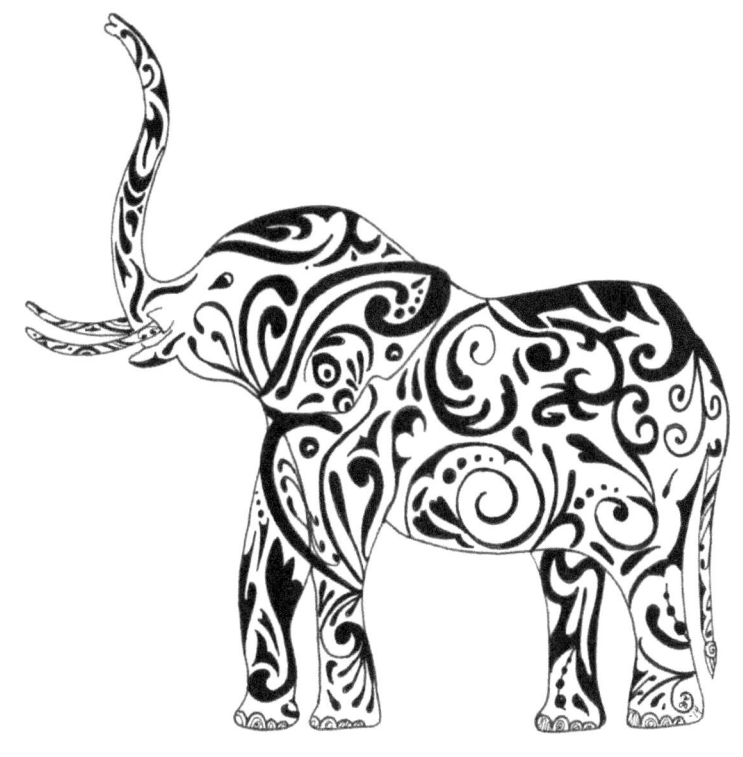

All pages are hand-drawn by:

Stacey Lynn Campbell-Milholland
Facebook & Etsy: Designs by Stacey Lynn

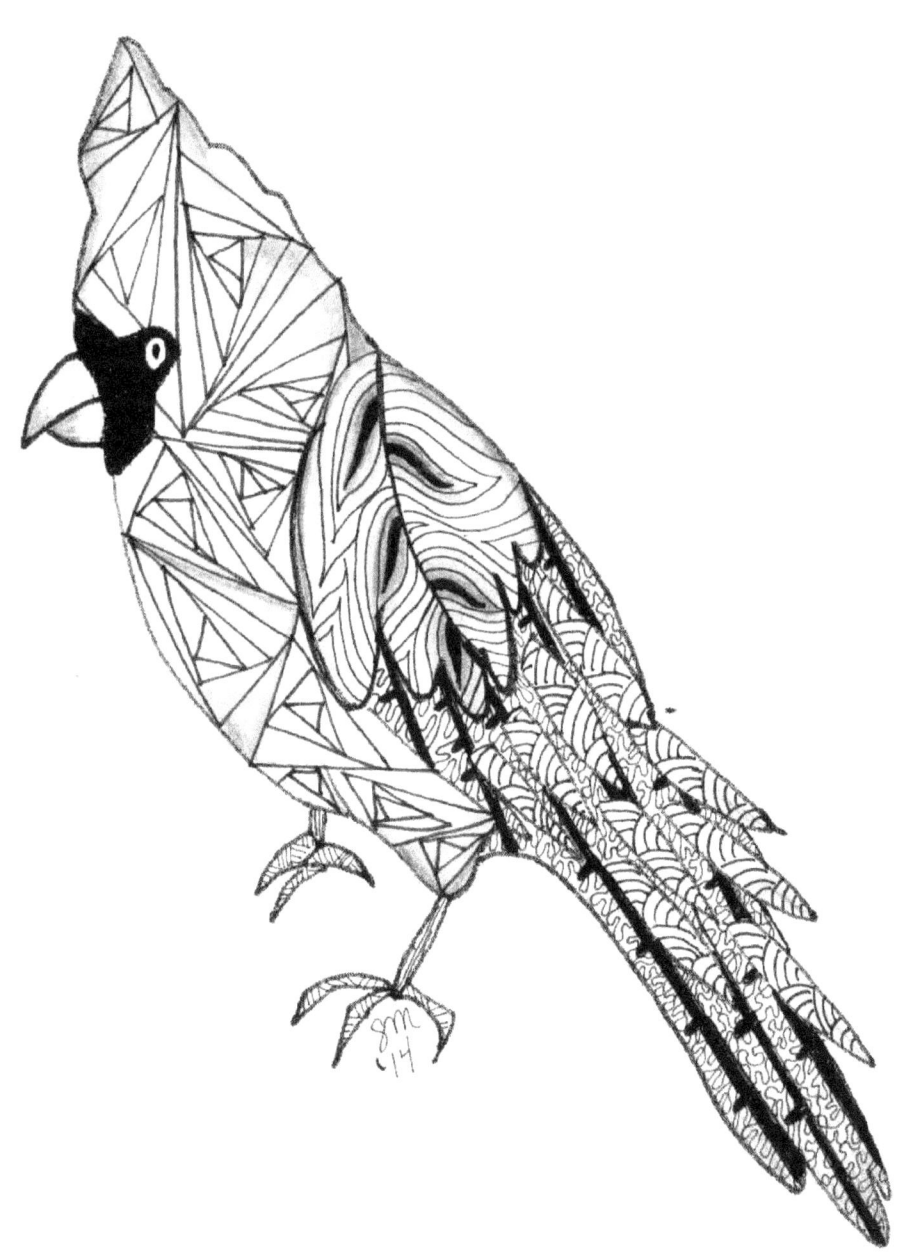

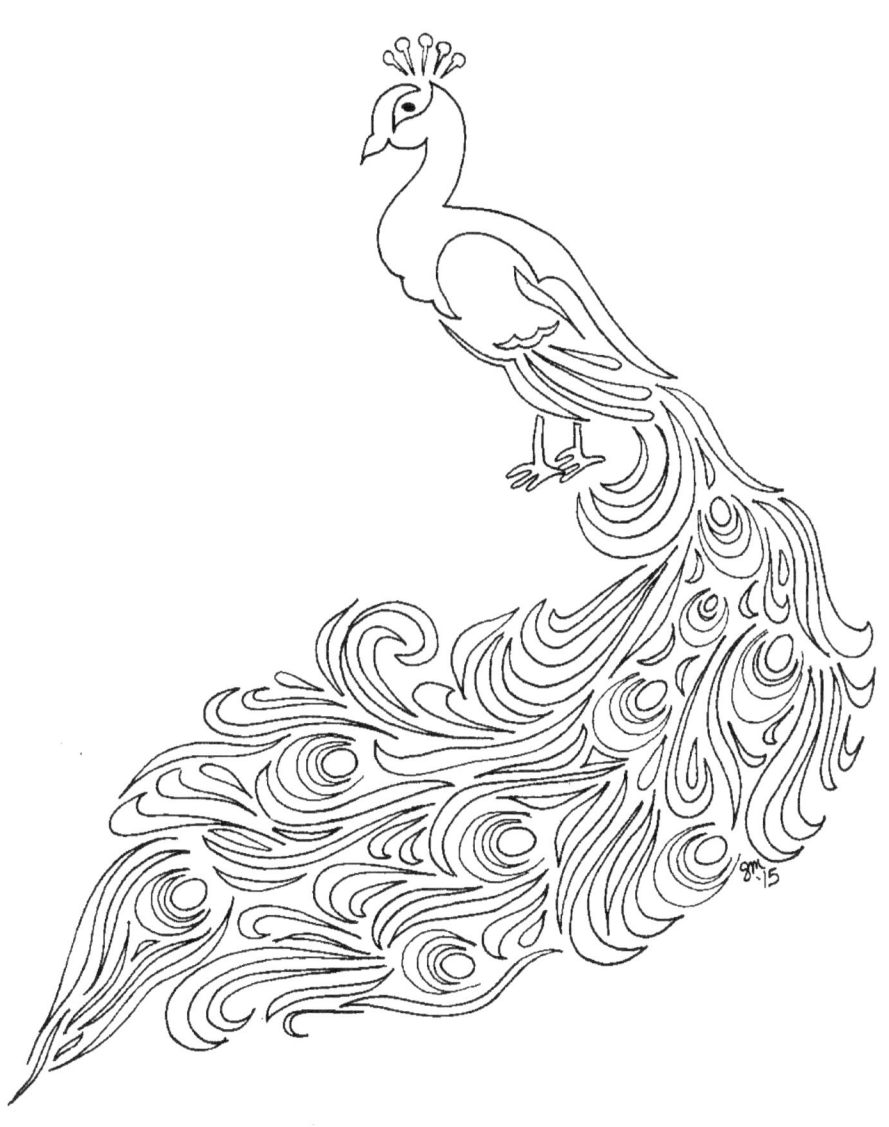

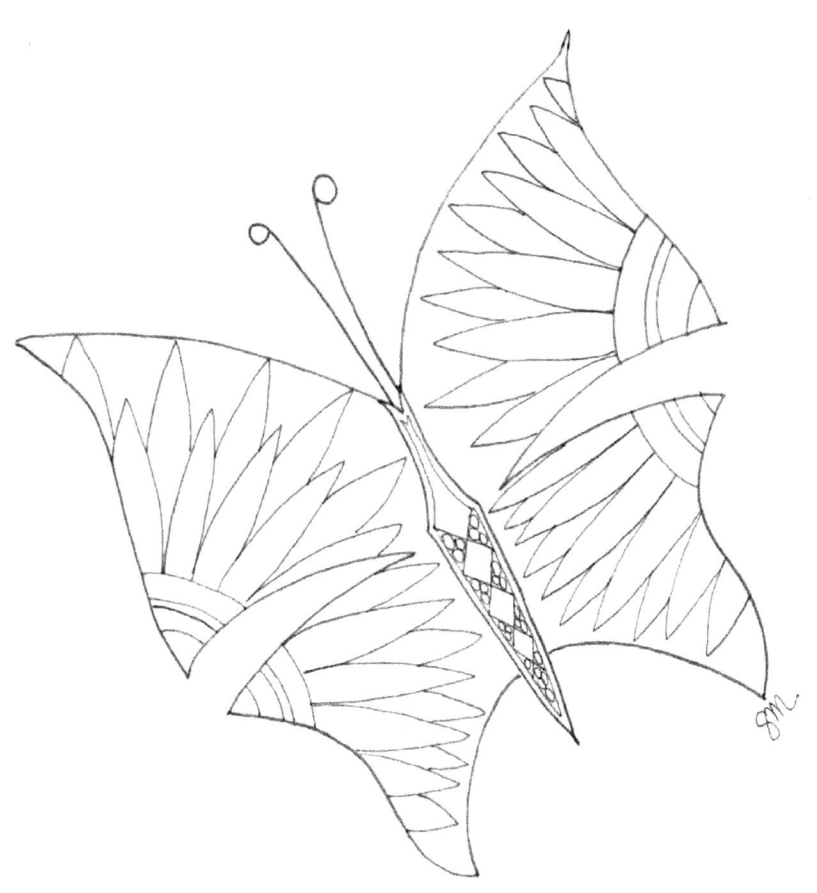

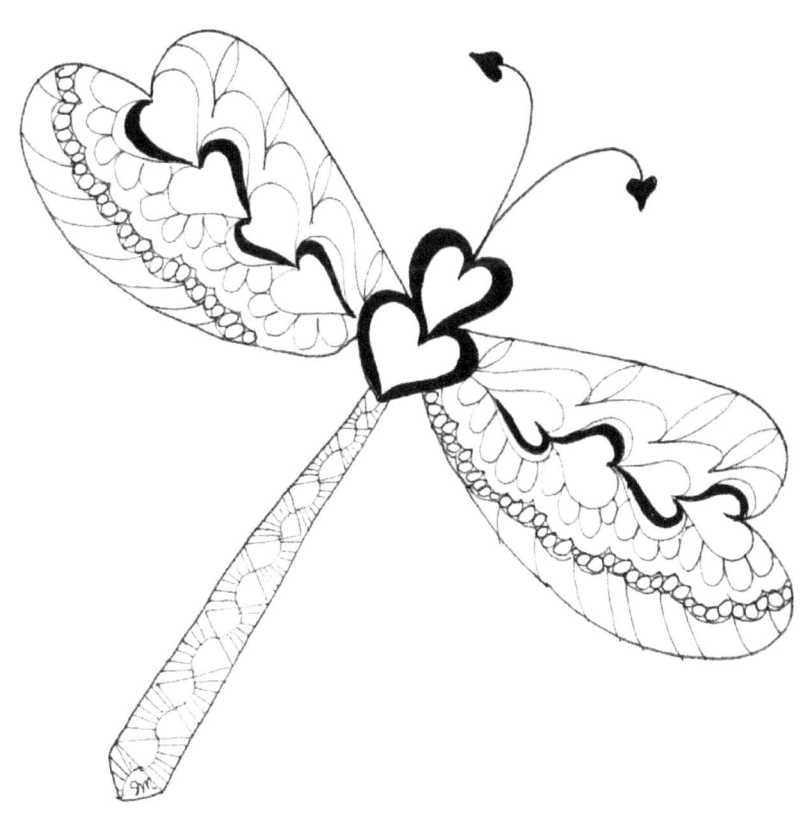

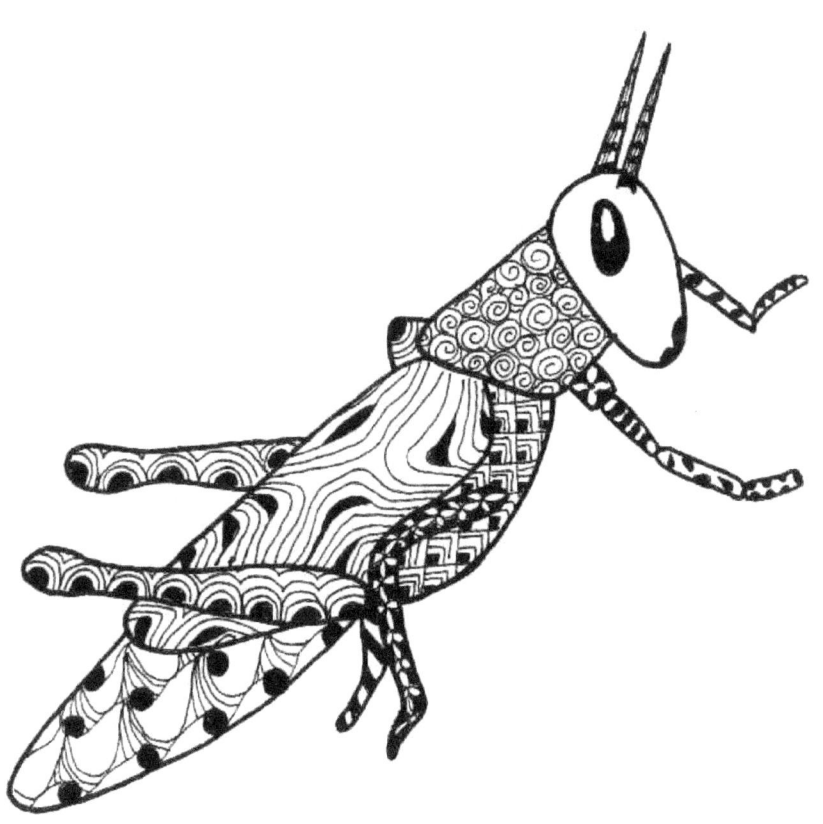

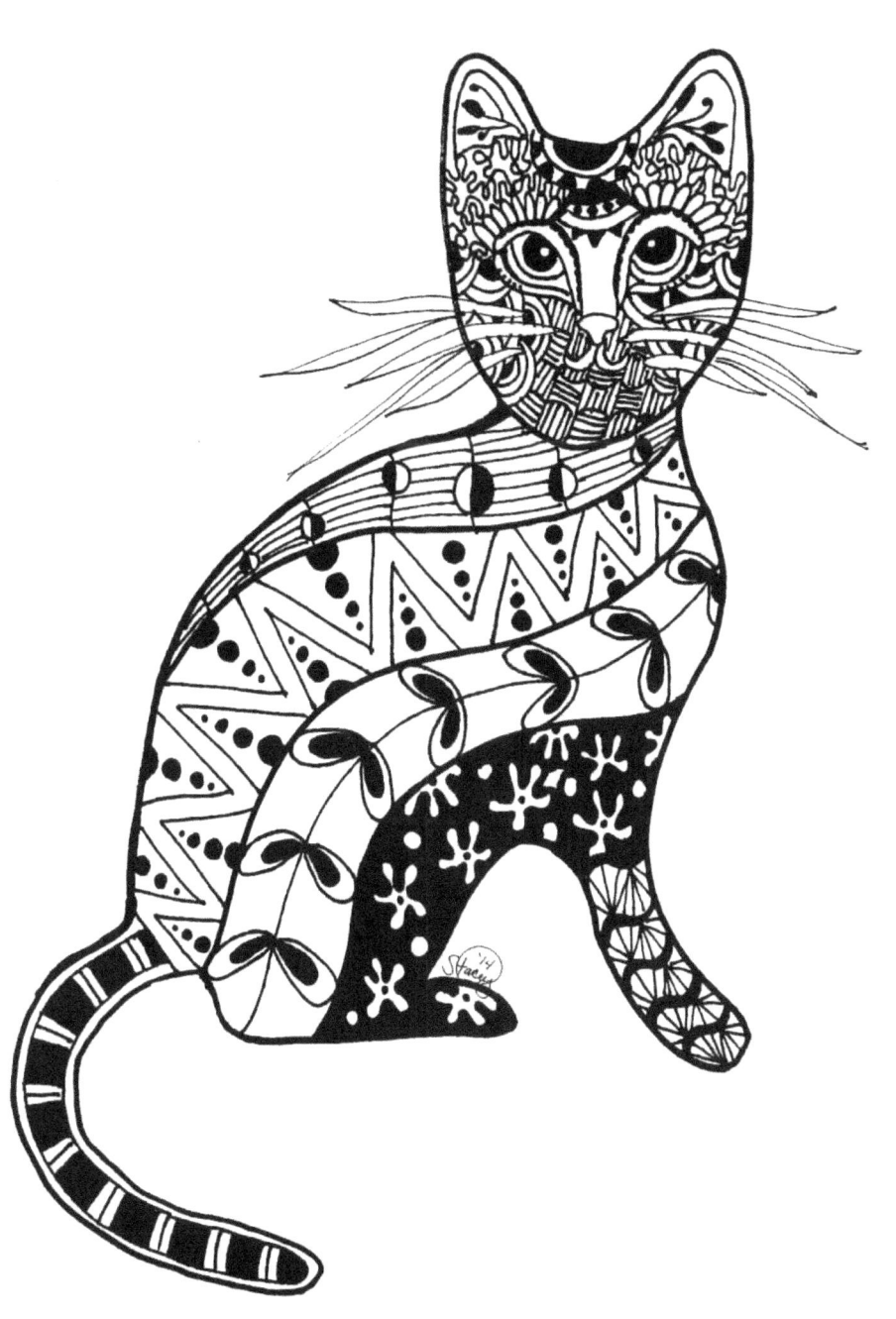

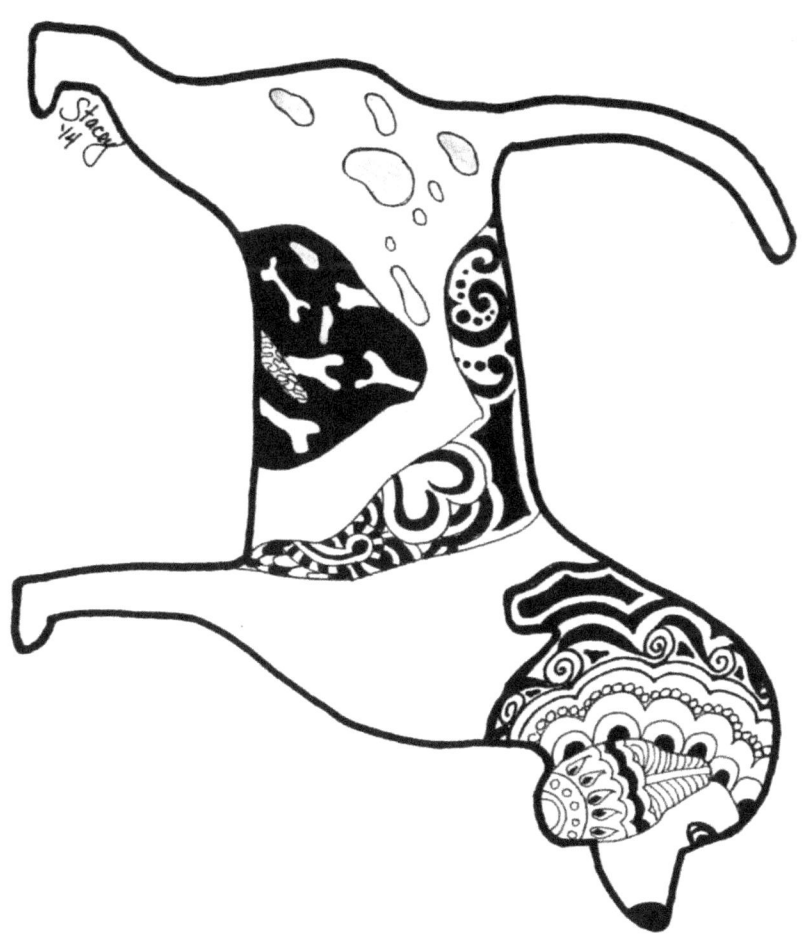

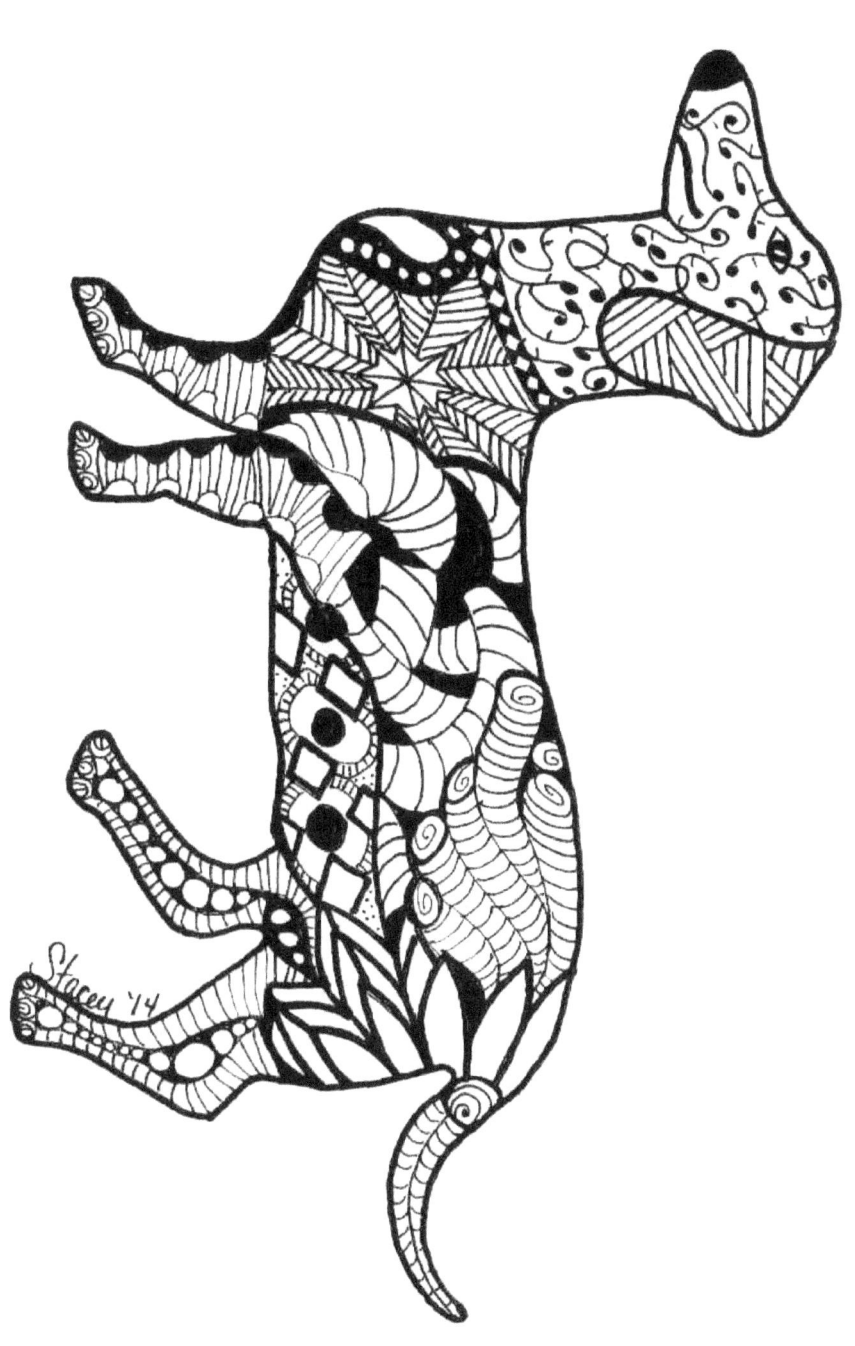

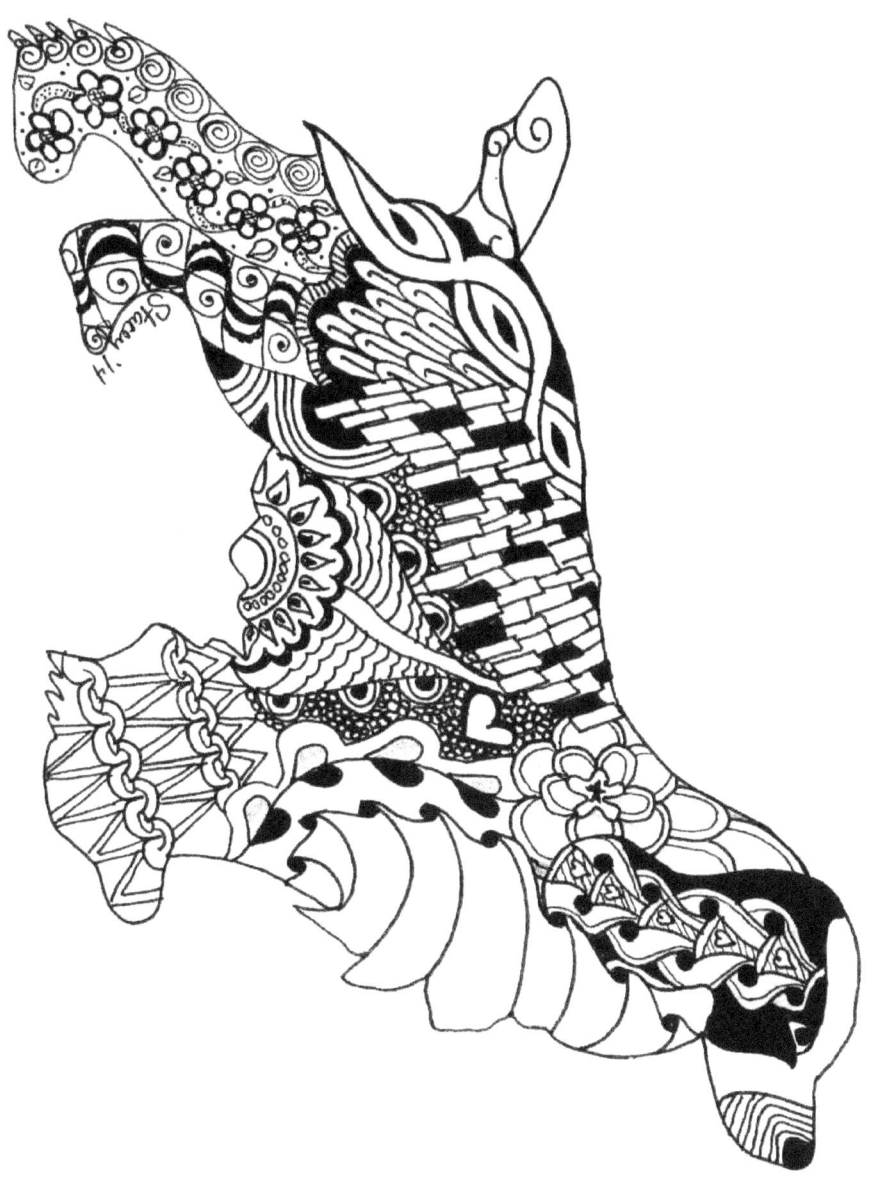

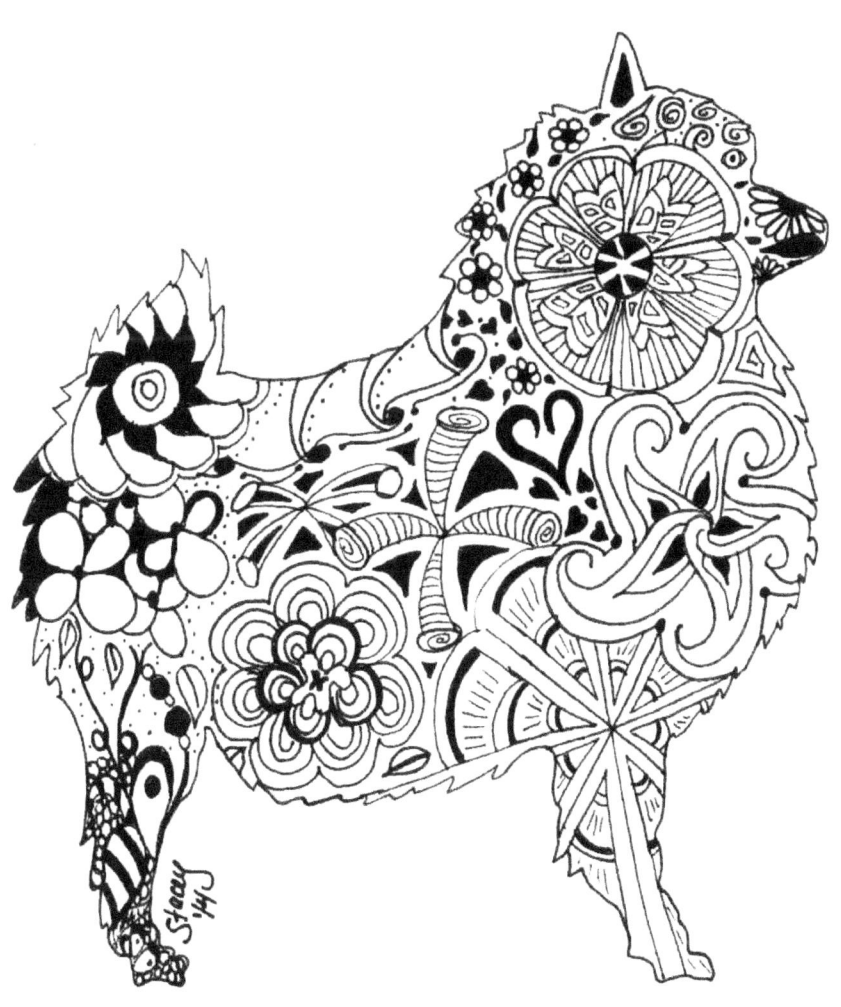

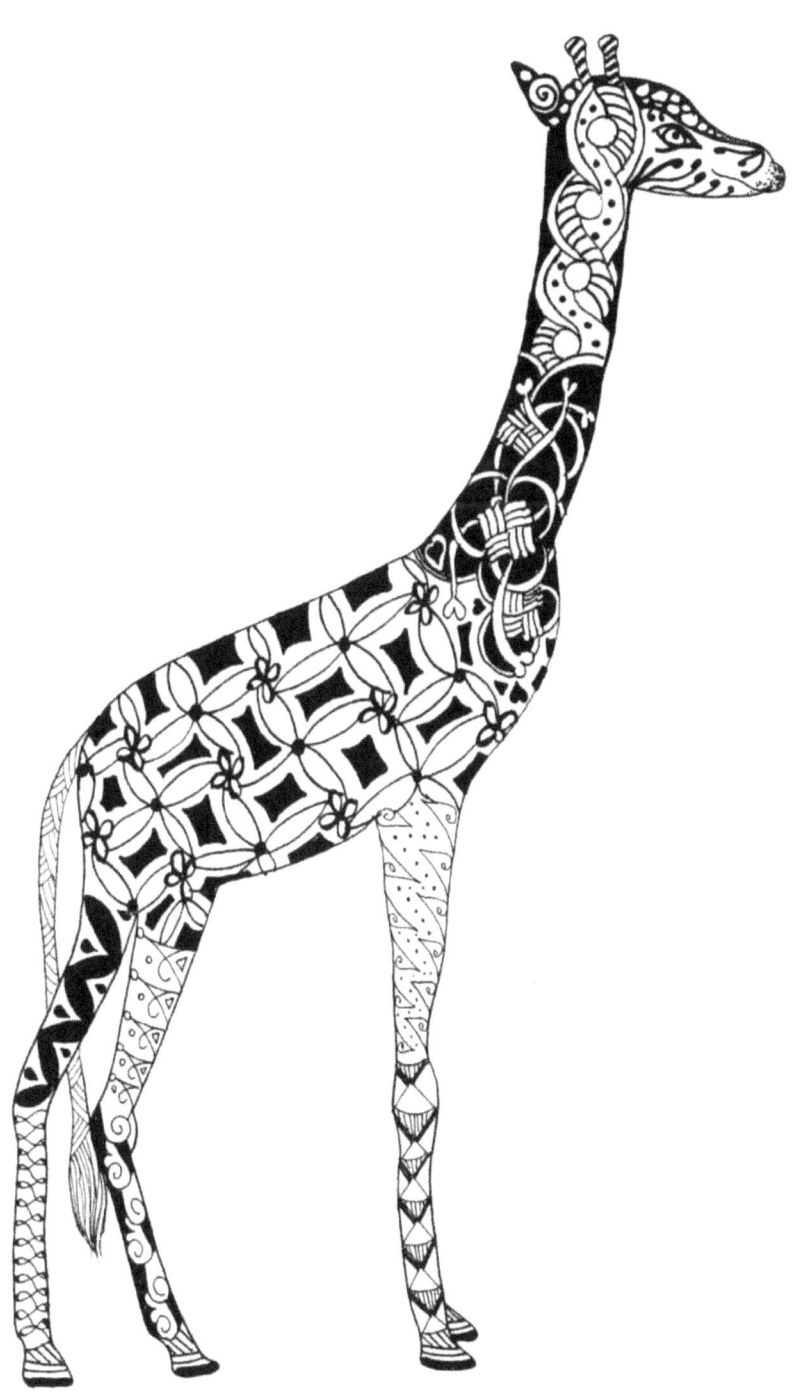

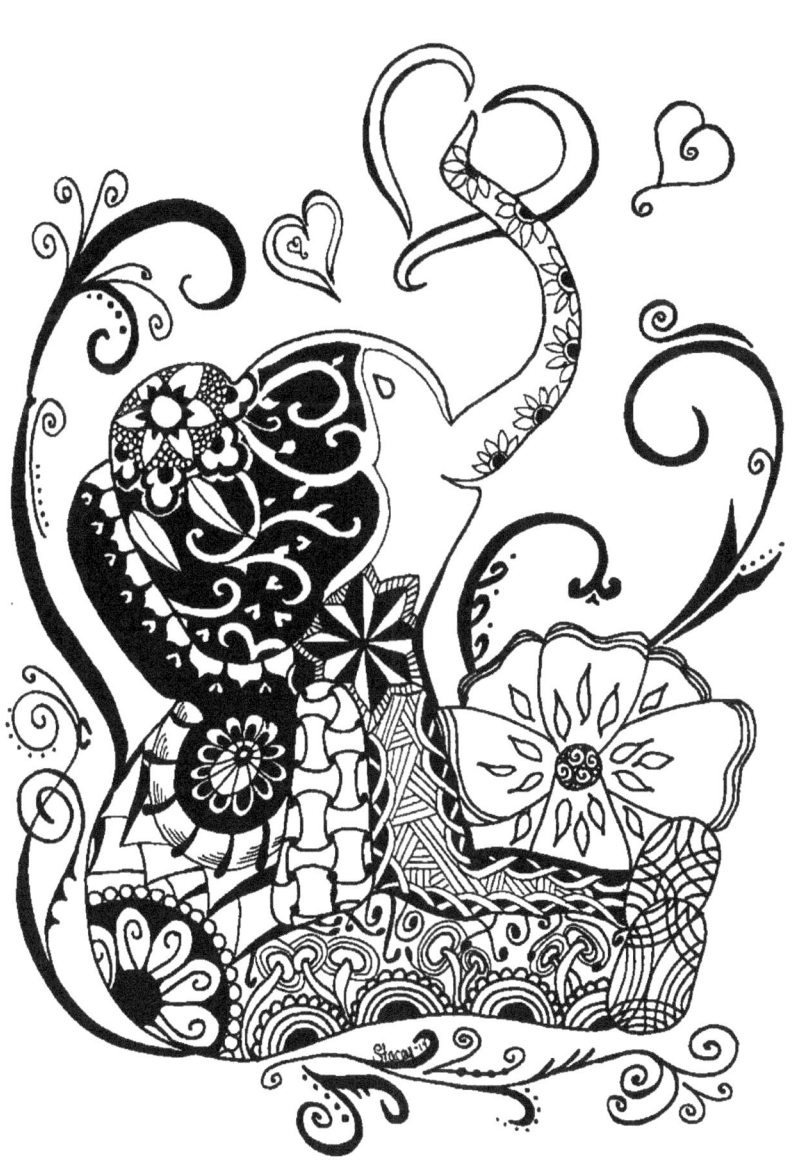

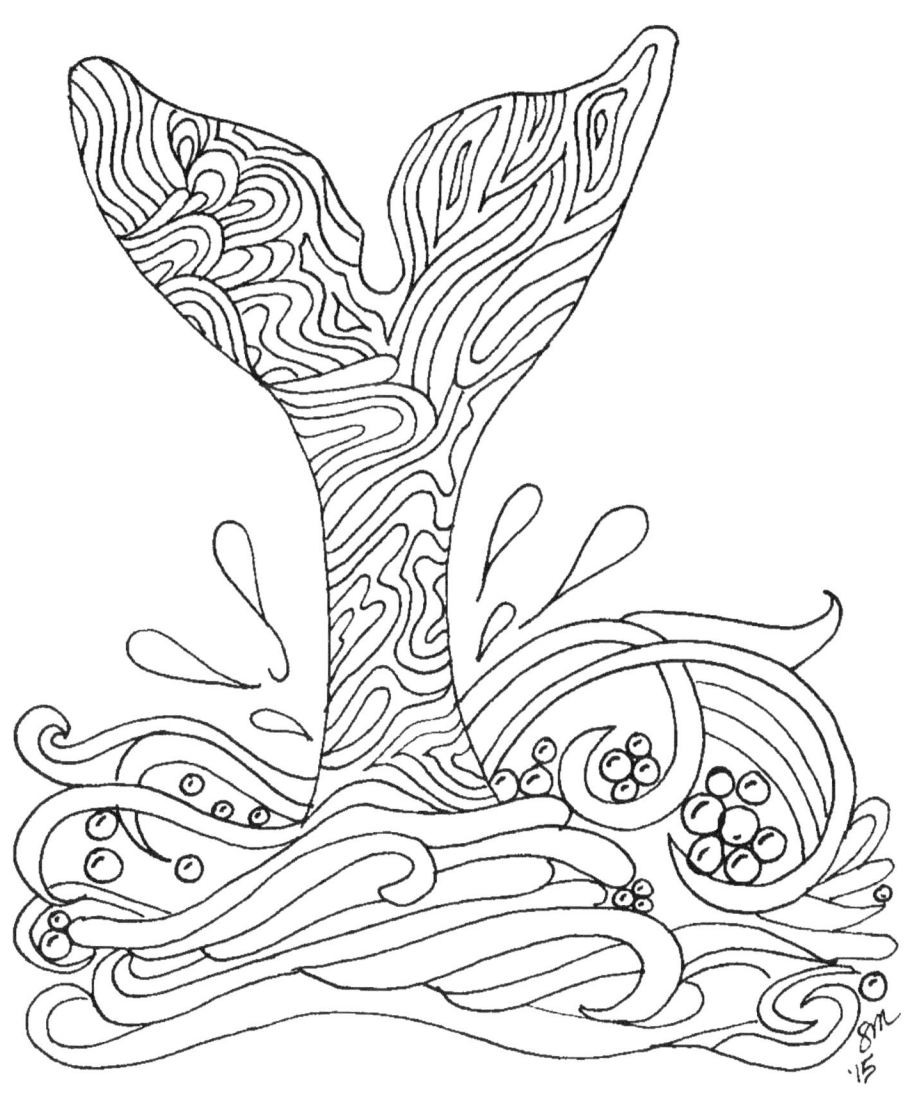

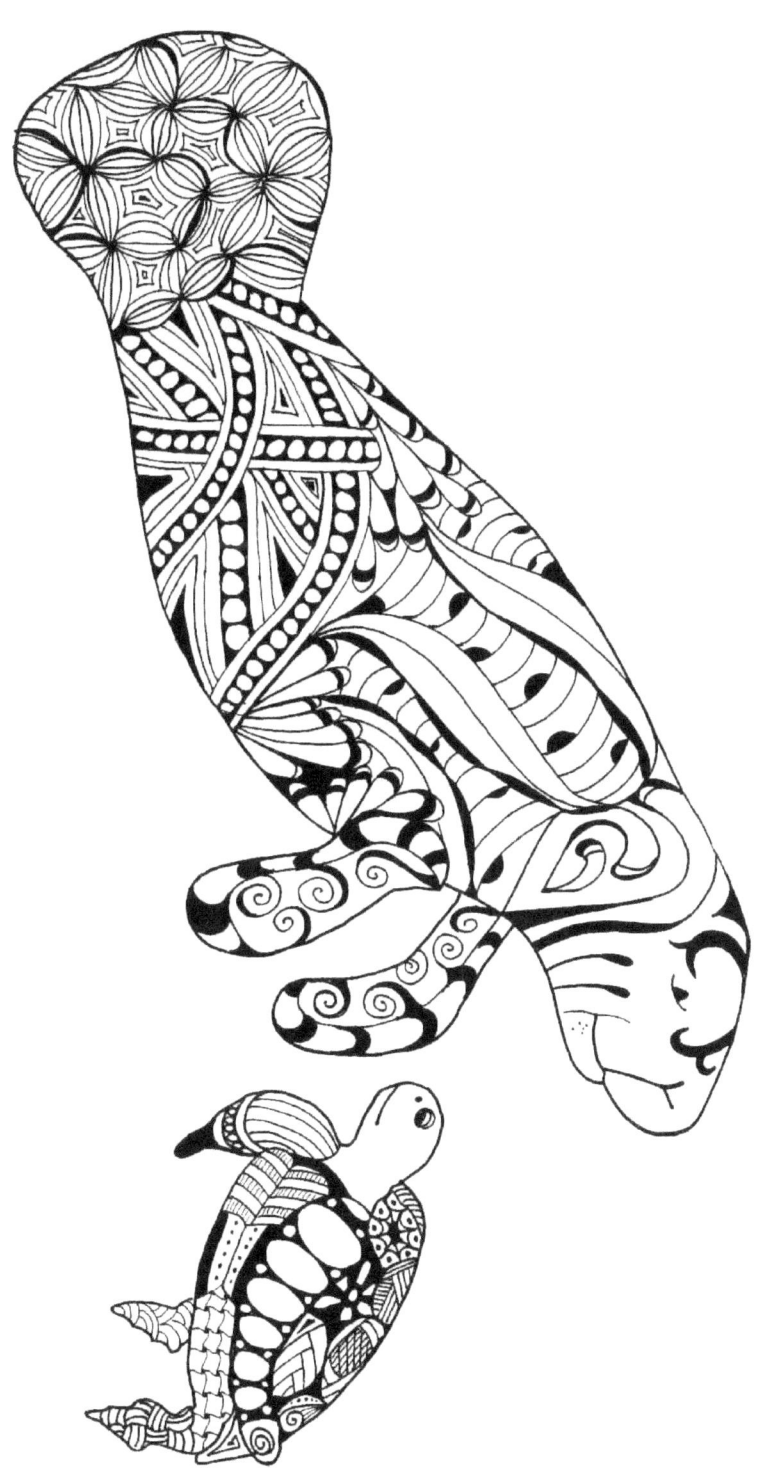

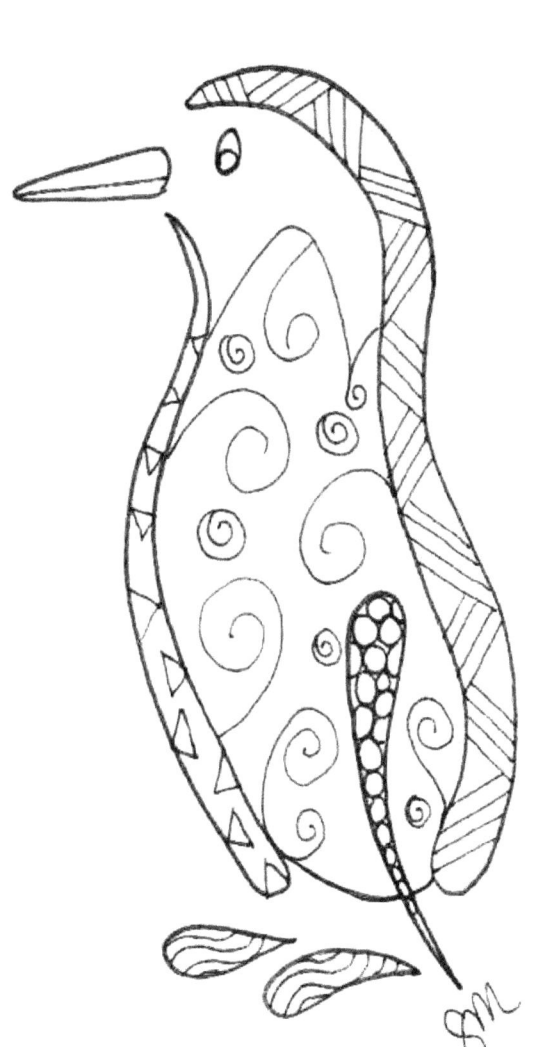

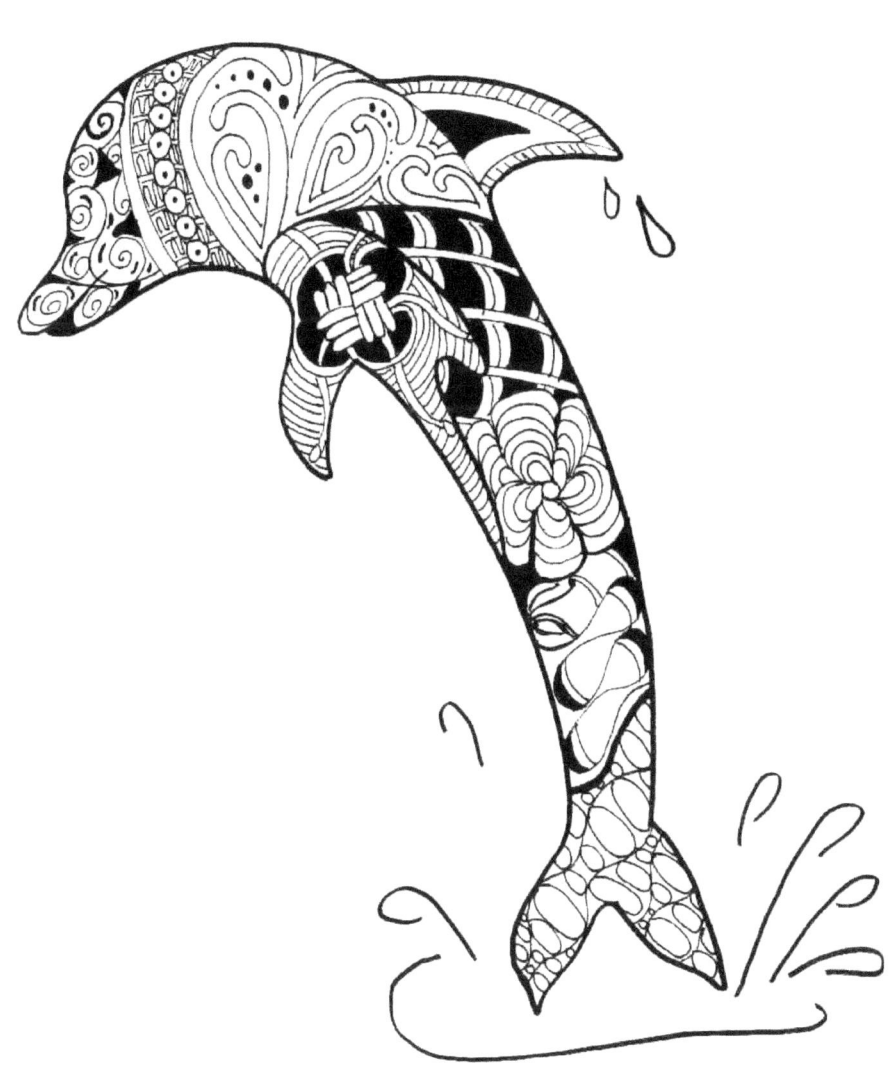

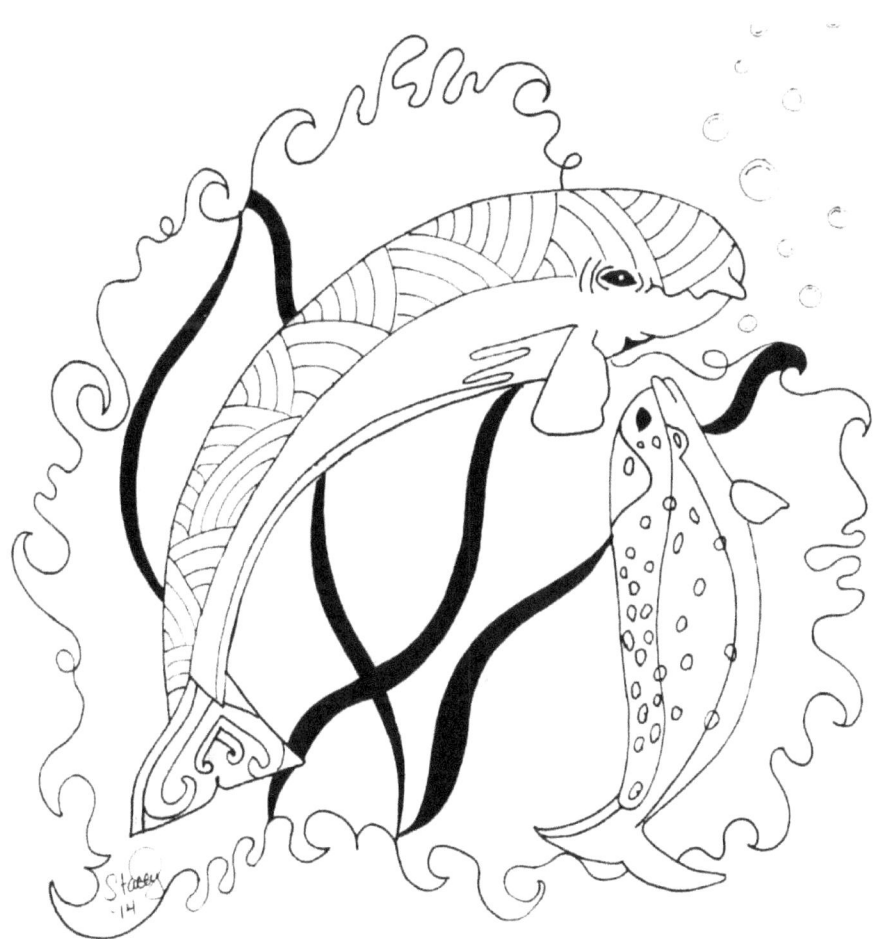

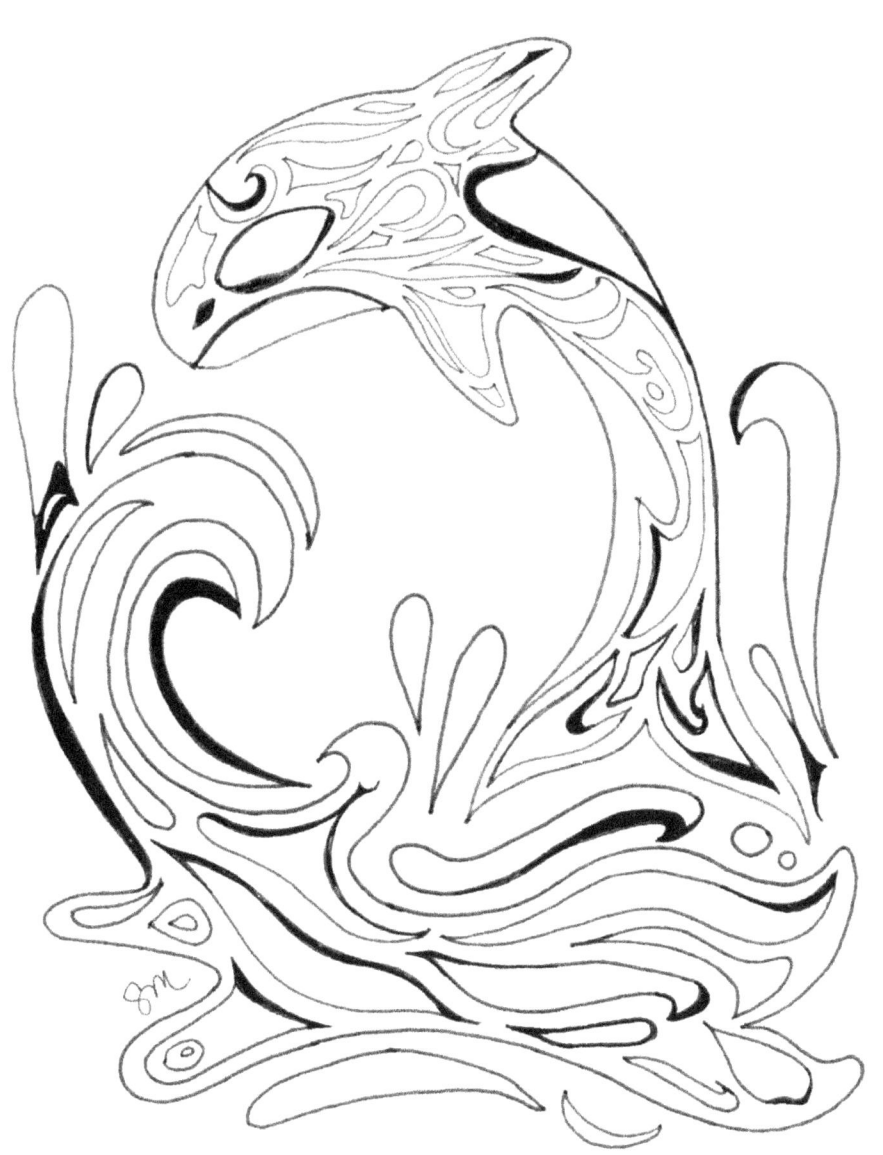

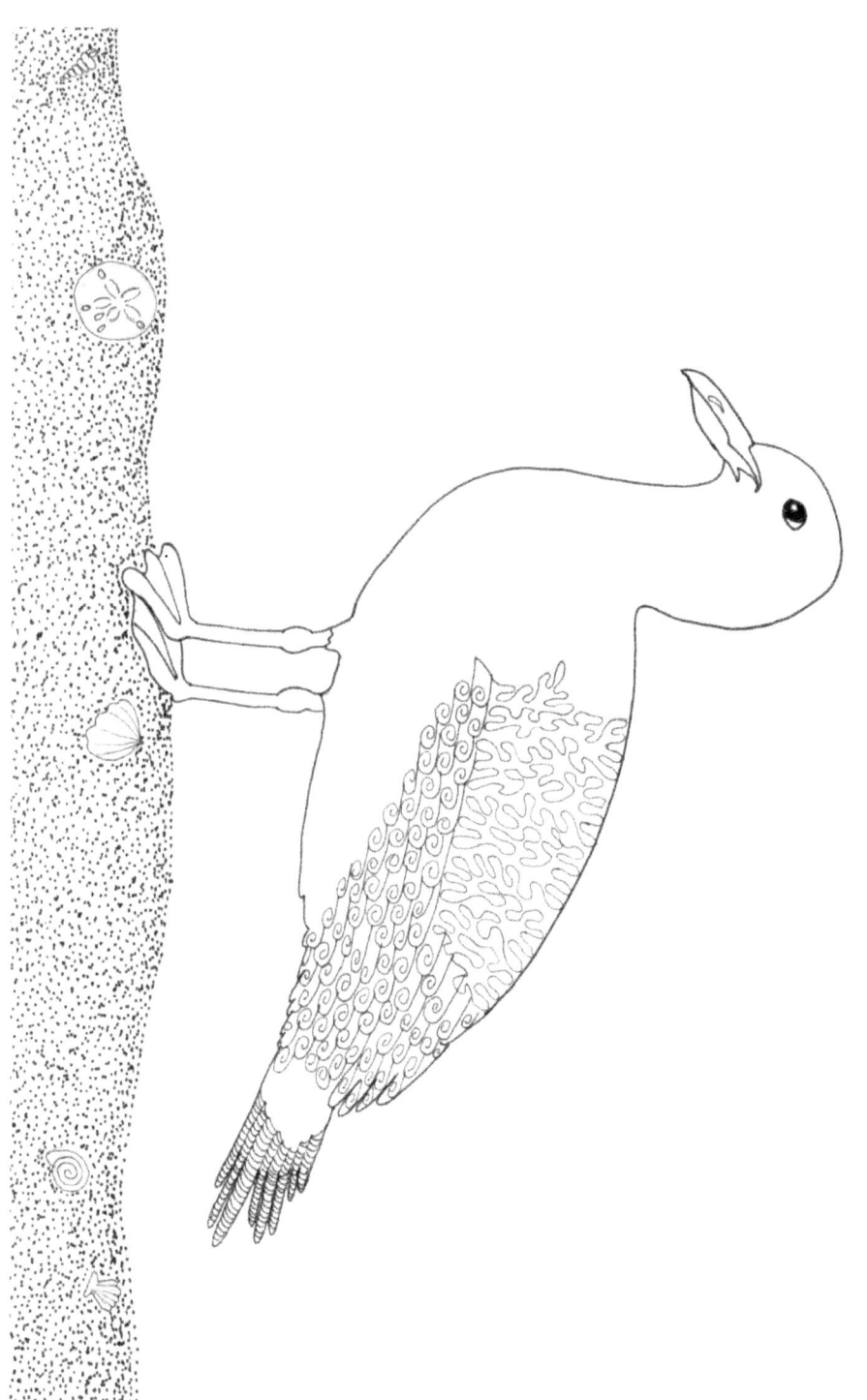

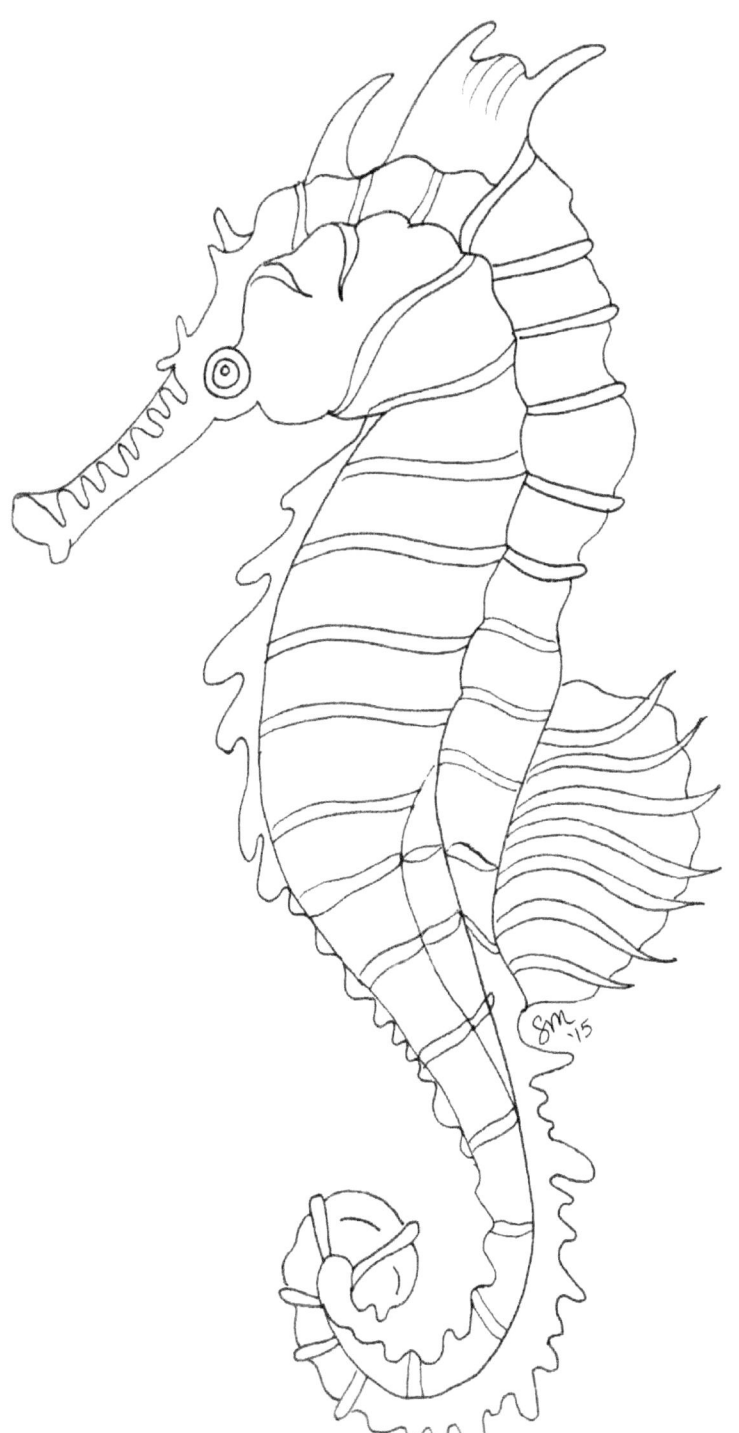